Child Survival
SKILLS

How to Detect and Avoid Dangerous People

Jerry Hyde
and
Terra Hulse

Illustrated by Sandra Kowallis

Bentle Books
Oakhurst, California

•

Disclaimer: Please note that the authors and publisher of this book are *not responsible* in any manner whatsoever for any injury that may result from practicing the techniques and/or following the instructions within. Although the authors and publisher have made every effort to ensure the accuracy and completeness of information contained in this book, we assume no responsibility for errors, inaccuracies, omissions, or any inconsistency herein. Any slights of people, places, or organizations are unintentional.

Illustrated by Sandra Kowallis, sky@usinternet.com, 559-298-6298

First printing 2004

ISBN 0-9746904-4-9
LCCN 2003115880

ATTENTION CORPORATIONS, UNIVERSITIES, COLLEGES, AND PROFESSIONAL ORGANIZATIONS: Quantity discounts are available on bulk purchases of this book for educational, gift purposes, or as premiums for increasing magazine subscriptions or renewals. Special books or book excerpts can also be created to fit specific needs. For information, please contact Bentle Books, P.O. Box 2274, Oakhurst, CA 93644; 559-692-2368; www.BentleBooks.com.

This book is dedicated
to all the missing children
and their families.

*"May the Lord bless you and keep you;
make his face shine upon you and be gracious to you;
turn his face toward you and give you peace."*

—Numbers 6:24–26

Table of Contents

Acknowledgments

To all the many people who work so hard to protect the lives of children: law enforcement agencies, social workers, counselors, researchers, and volunteers. Thank you for your hard work and dedication.

To the following people we offer our deepest heartfelt thanks for bringing this dream to fruition.

Terra Hulse, my co-author and one of my most dedicated students, who also had the dream and felt the urgency of this project and who sacrificed many hours of rest after long days at her job as a nurse to bring this book to completion.

Mike Hulse, who gave up valuable family time with his wife for her to work on this project.

Patsy Carpenter, my fiancee, my blessing, my love, who knew little about the martial arts when she met me, but looked into my heart and saw the flame that burned. She realized the importance of sharing the knowledge contained in this book with others. Her support, patience, prayers, encouragement, and understanding heart made this labor of love possible.

—Jerry Hyde

Thanks to my teacher and co-author, Jerry Hyde, for his commitment to teaching people of all ages how to protect themselves and trusting me to help him fulfill his dream of writing this book.

Thanks to my dear husband *Mike* for without his unconditional support and encouragement this book would never have had the chance to change so many lives.

Thanks to my son *Jacob,* who reminds me daily how precious children are and how important it is to protect them.

Thanks to all of *our family and friends* who continue to support this huge endeavor. We love and appreciate you very much.

—Terra Hulse

Foreword

No one wants to believe in evil; no one wants to believe that people can do harmful things to other people, especially children. But closing our eyes to it, not believing in it, doesn't make it go away. We live in a very violent time. We live in a world where horrible things happen each and every day. But we can and should remember that something can be done to help prevent at least some of these awful things from happening. We need to begin teaching our children how not to become victims. We need to begin the instruction today. Anything that brings us toward this goal should not only be considered but embraced. Not to do so is a crime in itself.

It's not just enough to applaud Master Jerry Hyde and Terra Hulse for their efforts to help our children remain safe. Every parent, martial arts instructor, public school teacher, aunt, uncle, and adult upon whom a child looks to for safety should buy this book, read this book, and then live this book until it becomes second nature. It is sad to think that the world has come to this, but it is idiocy to simply let it happen.

Hindsight is a luxury we cannot afford. Take steps now so that another child is not victimized, another family is not broken apart, and another precious life is not lost. There can be no greater need than to protect our children at any cost.

Emil Bautista
9th Degree Grand Master in Kajukenbo
Owner and Chief Instructor
Kajukenbo Self-Defense Institute of Vallejo, California

Introduction

The Why and How of It
Why You Need This Book

It is estimated . . .

- four million child molesters reside in the United States.

- a typical child molester will abuse 50 to 150 children before being arrested.

- thirty-four percent of all sexual assault victims reported to law enforcement agencies are under age 12.

- one in five children who uses the Internet regularly is asked to engage in sexual activity online.

- on average, 2,000 children are reported missing every day.

What would your child do or say if approached by a sexual predator? What if the person were a stranger, friend, or family member? Can your child recognize and avoid a dangerous situation at school, a public place, a friend's house—or even home? How can your child avoid viewing unwanted sexual images on the Internet? The "don't talk to strangers" advice is not enough. Your child needs specific instruction on what to look for, what to say, what to do, how to escape, where to run, who to tell, and what to tell.

Child Survival Skills is the tool you need to teach your children how to keep themselves safe from sexual predators. This interactive workbook opens the door of communication on the often unspoken topics of child molestation, exploitation, and abduction in a style that is not frightening but rather encouraging and empowering. Through these lessons, children will build their self-reliance and decrease their chance of becoming a victim.

How This Book Works

This book is designed to teach children, ages 6 through 12, the skills they need to avoid becoming the victim of a sexual predator. Each lesson begins with a brief section for the parent(s) to read—grandparents, teachers, and supervising adults, this section is for you. It outlines the objectives of the lesson and includes suggestions on how parent(s) can reinforce the child's learning. We strongly recommend you review the entire lesson so you understand the concepts being taught. Ten minutes is all you'll need to review each lesson, with the exception of lesson 6, which has additional information for parents. This will enable you to discuss the concepts and techniques with your child, greatly influencing your child's learning. After you have reviewed the lesson, have your child read the lesson and complete the activities. Of course, younger children will need more assistance with the lessons than older children.

The lessons include a variety of learning activities. Most of them can be done individually, but some may require adult participation. There are drawings, skits, word puzzles, matchups, and even run-around games children can do with each other or their parent(s). We have tried to make this workbook fun and enjoyable; however, the seriousness of the topic remains. We encourage parents to participate in the activities with their child as much as possible.

Once the child has completed the lesson, the parent(s) should review the learning objectives with the child to confirm that the techniques have been put to memory. The safety techniques learned in these lessons should become part of the child's normal self-protective behavior, just like looking both ways before crossing the road.

Lesson 1

The Dangerous Myths

Parents

All too often we tell our children "Don't talk to strangers," and we leave it at that. Most children do not understand what is meant by "stranger." Who is a stranger to them? Is it someone they have never seen before? What if they have seen the person talk to mommy a few times? What if the person knows the child's name? Children can be easily convinced someone is not a stranger to them, but rather an acquaintance. Once a child feels acquainted with someone, he becomes much more vulnerable to seduction, coercion, and trickery.

Children also believe a dangerous person, place, or thing has particular characteristics. They usually envision a dangerous stranger as an unkempt older man driving an old truck and lurking in a dark scary place. Believing these myths can actually increase your child's risk of danger. If your child has preconceived ideas that a stranger or dangerous person must look ugly, act mean, or lurk in dark scary places, she will be confused when someone who doesn't fit that stereotype attempts to hurt her or engage her in sexual activity. The fact is a dangerous person can be anyone—the scary stranger, the soccer coach, or the teenage boy who plays basketball with your son once in a while.

You can't tell by looking at someone if they may be dangerous to your child. *Your child* can't tell either. Looking out for particular types of people is not enough. This is where we start. In this lesson, your child will evaluate his own preconceived ideas of strangers or dangerous people (who we will refer to as unsafe people) and discover he can't tell if someone is unsafe as easily as he thinks.

Kids

Maybe you have heard your parents or teachers tell you to keep away from strangers. Sometimes the word stranger is used to mean an unsafe person, but strangers are just people you do not know well. Most strangers are nice. Most people are nice to children, but there are some people who try to hurt children.

In this book, you are going to learn about two different types of people—**unsafe** people and **safe** people. A **safe** person makes you feel comfortable and never threatens you or tries to hurt you. An **unsafe** person is someone who may hurt you. An **unsafe** person may threaten you or just make you feel uncomfortable. In this lesson, you are going to learn more about **unsafe** people.

The **Unsafe** Quiz

Directions: Answer the following questions. Take your time. Write everything you can think of.

1. Do you think you could tell if someone is an unsafe person by just looking at them? _____

    _____

    _____

2. What would an unsafe person look like? Write lots of words to describe them. _____

    _____

    _____

3. What kind of car do you think an unsafe person would be driving? _____

    _____

    _____

4. Where do you think you would see an unsafe person? _____

    _____

    _____

5. If an unsafe person came up to you, what would he or she say?

    _____

    _____

    _____

The **Unsafe** Picture

Directions: Draw a picture of what you think an unsafe person would look like. You can draw more than one picture if you want to. Try to draw this person's clothes too. Use colors if you can.

The **Dangerous** Myths

Myths are things people believe that are not true. Compare your quiz answers to the *myths*. Then read the *truth*. *Truth* is what is real. The *truth* is the correct answer to the question.

MYTH: You can always tell if someone is an unsafe person because they will look dirty and scary. (This isn't true.)

Color the picture and learn the truth.

The Truth

We often think we could recognize an unsafe person. We usually picture the unsafe person as a dirty old stranger. However, the unsafe person is not always an old, dirty stranger. In fact, the unsafe person may be clean and friendly. It could be someone who looks and smells very nice. It could even be someone we know and like.

MYTH: The unsafe person will be a grown man. (This isn't always true.)

Color the picture and learn the truth.

The Truth

The unsafe person is not always a grown man. It is sometimes a woman. It may even be a teenager or an older kid. It could be a boy or a girl you know. It could be someone you have even played with out on the basketball court or at the park.

MYTH: The unsafe person will be driving an old truck or car. (No, this isn't correct either.)

Color the picture and learn the truth.

The Truth

Do you think an unsafe person may be around when you spot an old truck or car? That may be true, but what if the unsafe person decided to drive his convertible red sports car that day? Would you think the same thing about a nice sports car? The type of car someone drives does not tell you if the person is unsafe or not. An unsafe person can be driving anything or maybe nothing at all. Maybe the person just walked to the area where you are playing. So looking for a *certain kind* of car or truck doesn't help you spot an unsafe person.

MYTH: Unsafe people are only in bad places. (Unfortunately not.)

Color the picture
and learn the truth.

The Truth

Unsafe people are not only in bad scary places. They can be anywhere anytime. Even though staying out of places that you know are dangerous is very smart, you also need to remember unsafe people can be anywhere. They can be at the mall, church, playground, ball game, or even come to your own house.

MYTH: An unsafe person will be mean. (This isn't entirely true.)

Color the picture and learn the truth.

The Truth

Unsafe people might be very nice to you when they first meet you. Sometimes they will try to be extra nice to you. At first they may try to be your friend, buy you presents, or take you to fun places. They may ask you to help them look for something or find someone. Unsafe people like to trick kids this way.

Important Words

Directions: Write the definition of the words below. You can look back in the lesson if you have to. The important thing is that you understand what these words mean because you will see them a lot in lessons to come.

Unsafe person: _____

_____

_____

Safe person: _____

_____

_____

Stranger: _____

_____

_____

Myth: _____

_____

_____

Truth: _____

_____

_____

You did a great job in this lesson.
Now go tell someone what you have learned so far!

Lesson 2

Awareness

Someone is behind me.

Parents

In order to stay away from danger, you and your child must know how to identify its presence. We learned in the last lesson you can't tell if people are dangerous by looking at them, by what they are driving, or by expecting them to be mean. So what do you watch for?

Child predators use varied tactics to manipulate children. When the predator is a stranger to the child, he or she will often use trickery, threats, or force. When he is an acquaintance of the child, he will attempt to lower the child's inhibitions by offering the child gifts or attention. If the predator is someone within the family, he or she will often use his or her private access and authority to control the child.

What you should watch for is potentially dangerous *situations* or *actions* rather than particular types of people. We call these particular situations or actions *red flags.* These red flags are specific warning signs of danger. In this lesson, you and your child will learn how to identify the red flags associated with strangers.

Being aware of red flags in your environment is the first step to staying safe. Awareness, paying attention to what is going on around you, should be natural. You do it every day. You look for cars before you cross the street. You look to see how deep the water is before you dive in. Looking for red flags that may appear during your daily activities should be just as natural. All the red flags discussed in this lesson apply to both children and adults. You and your child should learn to recognize these red flags.

There is another aspect to awareness we will also cover in this lesson. This second aspect involves paying attention to details. Children will be taught how to recognize identifying characteristics of a suspicious person and identifying marks of a suspicious vehicle. Being able to give detailed information to the authorities regarding suspicious persons or vehicles may aid in the capture of a kidnapper or child molester. It may even save the life of another child.

You too must pay attention to details. You should be aware of what your child was wearing last. Photographs should be taken of your child four times per year so you always have a recent picture. This is especially important with younger children. Make note of any distinguishing characteristics of your child, such as birthmarks, moles, scars, or any other specific features. Your child's fingerprints should be taken as well. Contact your local law enforcement agency to have this done. Most importantly, you should know where your children are and who they are with at all times.

Before your child begins this lesson, remind him that these lessons should not frighten him. There is no need to be afraid. The goal of these lessons is to teach him how to stay away from dangerous situations (just like not crossing the street when a car is coming). Talk to your child in a calm and simple way. Let him know he can talk to you if he has any fears or questions. Listen to his concerns and answer his questions. Remember, children who feel they do not have anyone to talk to at home are more vulnerable to exploitation and abduction. At the end of this lesson, there is a page titled *More Practice.* This page is full of additional activities you and your child can do together to reinforce the concepts taught in this lesson.

Part One: The Red Flags

Kids

We learned in the last lesson you can't tell if someone is **unsafe** by looking at him or her. You learned that an **unsafe** person could be a man, a woman, or even an older kid. He or she could be driving any type of vehicle or maybe just leaning up against a tree on your way home. You also learned he or she could be almost anyplace. So how are you going to be able to tell an **unsafe** person from a **safe** person? How are you going to know if someone is dangerous to you? In this lesson, we are going to teach you the things you can and should be watching for. We call these things *red flags*.

Red flags are **danger signs**. They are important clues that can alert you to danger. These *red flags* should not make you scared. They are just warning signals. When you see them, you must pay close attention to your safety. Knowing how to spot a *red flag* can keep you out of danger. It is just like looking for cars before you cross the street. You must look in all directions to make sure no cars are coming your way. The same goes for these *red flags*. Pay attention to what is going on around you, so you can spot them when they are there.

Common Red Flags for All the Time

Red flag: Feeling uncomfortable or scared.

Pay attention to your feelings. If you feel uncomfortable or afraid, this is a warning something may be wrong. Trust yourself.

Red flag: Someone older than you, who you do not know, asks for your help.

Unsafe people like to trick kids. They may ask you to help them find something, such as a lost puppy. They may ask you to help them find the pizza place. They may even offer you money or a gift in exchange for your help. An adult or even an older kid should not be asking you for help or directions. They should be asking an adult for help. Even if they really seem to need help, it is not safe for you to try to help them.

Red flag: Someone offering you money or gifts.

Unsafe strangers offer things like gifts and money to trick kids into going with them.

Red flag: Someone asking to take your picture.

No one should ask you if he or she could take your picture. This person should ask your parents.

Red flag: Someone trying to touch you in the parts of your body that would be covered by a bathing suit.

The parts of your body that are covered by a bathing suit are private areas. No one should touch those areas of your body, and you should not touch those areas on someone else's body.

Red Flags at Public Places

When you are at a game, the store, a playground, or any large group gathering, watch for the following *red flags*.

Red flag: Someone watching you too long.

If someone, especially an adult, is watching you too much and making you feel uncomfortable, this is a red flag.

Red flag: An adult who doesn't seem to belong in your area.

If you notice someone who doesn't seem to belong in your area, such as a man hanging around the playground who doesn't have any kids with him, this is a red flag.

Red flag: Any person you don't know coming toward you.

If someone you do not know is walking toward you, this is a red flag. Unfortunately, you can't tell a safe person from an unsafe person by looking at him or her, so it's safest to avoid letting this person get close to you.

Red Flags Outside

While walking, playing, or riding your bike outside, watch for the following *red flags*.

Red flag: Any vehicle that stops along the curb, either in front or behind you, while you are walking along the sidewalk.

Sometimes unsafe people park their cars alongside the road to wait for an unsuspecting kid to walk by. Watch for any vehicle that stops near you. Listen for the sound of cars slowing down behind you.

Red flag: Anyone getting out of a vehicle and standing next to it in an area near or in the path you must walk.

If someone you do not know is standing in the path you must walk, this is a red flag. This stranger may be dangerous and it is unsafe for you to go near them.

Red flag: Anyone who gets out of a vehicle and begins to walk toward you.

As you learned before, it is better to be safe and avoid him or her.

Red flag: Anyone opening the door of a vehicle near your path.

If you do not know this person, you do not know if he or she is safe. Pay attention to him. Just in case, he is waiting for you to come close to him.

Red flag: Anyone in a vehicle who appears to be watching you.

If someone in a vehicle is watching you, making you uncomfortable, this is a red flag.

Red flag: A vehicle with its motor still running.

If a vehicle nearby has its motor still running, keep your distance. Leaving the vehicle motor on enables the driver to get away more quickly. Some unsafe people do this when they are going to do something bad.

Red flag: Anyone leaning against a tree or wall in your path.

Sometimes unsafe people wait for kids to walk by along a path.

Red Flags for Public Bathrooms

When you need to use the bathroom at the park, movies, shopping center, sports arena, or any other public place, watch for the following red flags:

 Red flag: Being alone in the bathroom.

 Red flag: Anyone who was previously sitting or standing nearby and now walks toward the bathroom when you do.

 Red flag: Anyone you don't know trying to talk to you in the bathroom.

Unsafe people like to go to isolated places such as bathrooms to do bad things. You should not go to the bathroom alone. If no one is in the bathroom with you, an unsafe person could try to hurt you there. If someone you do not know seems to be following you, especially to a less crowded place like the bathroom, pay attention. It is also not safe to talk to someone you do not know while in the bathroom.

Red Flags While in the Car

When you are in the car with an adult, watch for the following red flags:

Red flag: Someone in the car parked next to you gives you a bad feeling or worries you.

Anytime you have a bad feeling or something worries you, it is a red flag.

Red flag: Someone is following you in another vehicle.

If you suspect someone is following you in another vehicle, tell the driver of the car you are in right away.

Red flag: Being told to wait in the car alone.

You should never wait alone in a car. Being alone in a public place is always a red flag.

Red flag: Parking in a dark area.

Staying in a lighted area is safer. Unsafe people sometimes avoid lighted areas.

Red flag: Someone in another vehicle is looking at you or anyone in the car with you too long.

Remember someone staring at you too long is always a red flag.

Red Flags Activity

Look at the pictures below. Explain how each picture could be a red flag.

Part Two: Paying Attention to Details

Kids

What if you noticed a stranger, sitting in a car near where you and your friends like to play? This person was watching you and your friends, and you felt uncomfortable. You wanted to tell your parents or the police about this person. What would you tell them? Could you give a detailed description of the person or the car? In this part of the lesson, you are going to learn what things you can quickly look for to be able to identify a person or vehicle. Learning how to give a detailed description of a person or vehicle may help the police find an unsafe person.

Identifying a Stranger

Here is a list of several things you can use to give a more detailed description of people:

● Is the person male or female?

● What kind of clothing are they wearing (colors, jeans, dress, hat, etc.)?

● What kind of shoes are they wearing (tennis shoes, boots, sandals, etc.)?

● Do they have any tattoos? (Where was it and what did it look like?)

● Do they have any special facial characteristics (mustache, scars, moles, etc.)?

● Are they wearing glasses?

● What does their hair look like (brown, black, blonde, pink, long, short, buzzed, bobbed)?

● What color is their skin (dark, light)?

● What color are their eyes (blue, brown, green)?

● How tall are they? (You can tell this by comparing where their head is to things near them, such as a light post, top of a car, or a doorway. Then later you can have the police officer, or whoever is getting the information from you, stand in the same place you saw the suspicious person and compare heights.)

● Are they thin, heavy, or muscular?

● Is there anything unusual about their walk? (Do they have a limp, drag their feet, walk fast or slow, or use a cane?)

Identify the Stranger

In this activity, you are going to identify characteristics of the strangers. This will help you learn the different things that can make someone unique. Unique means unlike anyone else. Draw a line from the words to the object(s) they describe. You can also color the picture to remind yourself to pay attention to colors too.

Men

baseball cap   glasses   light-colored hair   earring   ponytail

sweat suit   work uniform   shorts   tattoo   freckles

shirt with #10 on front

business suit

toolbox

briefcase

cigarette

tall

necktie

dark hair

dark skin   tank top   sunglasses   mustache

hairy chest   light skin   tennis shoes   dress shoes

Women

Draw a line from the words to the object(s) they describe. You can also color the picture to remind yourself to pay attention to colors too.

light-colored hair   dark hair   dress   dark eyes   dark skin

light skin   short hair   long hair   earrings   curly hair

sunglasses

spiked multicolored hair

glasses

thin

heavy   tall   short   high heels   sandals

boots   skirt   tattoo   nose ring

Teenagers

Draw a line from the words to the object(s) they describe. You can also color the picture to remind yourself to pay attention to colors too.

light hair   dark hair   glasses   baseball cap

Tigers Gym shirt   earring   muscular   thin

dark skin

light skin

sunglasses

long hair

tank top

shorts

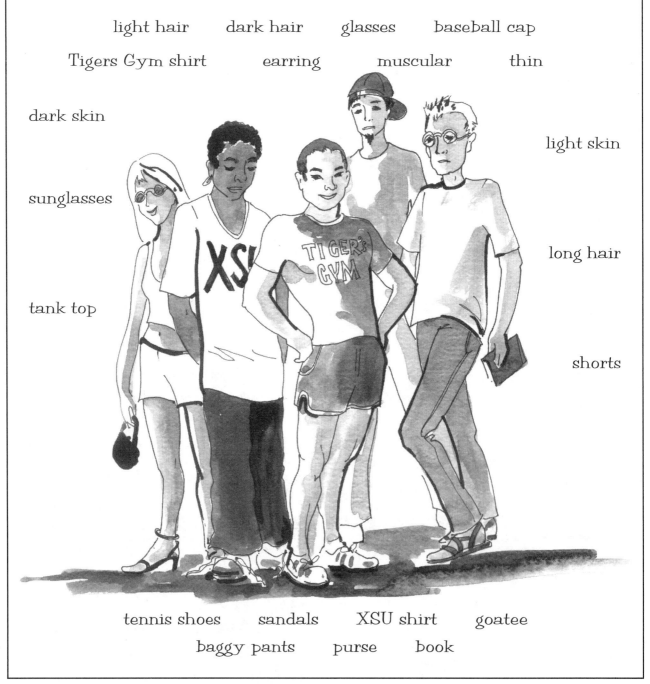

tennis shoes   sandals   XSU shirt   goatee

baggy pants   purse   book

Identifying a Vehicle

Here is a list of things you can use to help identify a vehicle:

- Color of the vehicle (standard one color, two-toned, primer, pen striping, special lettering)
- Windows—tinted, broken, cracked
- Type of truck—single cab, extended cab, camper shell, 4x4
- Type of SUV—large, small, etc.
- Type of car—2 door, rear door, compact, convertible, sedan, luxury
- Type of van—mini, full size
- Vehicle damage—dents, scratches, missing parts
- License plate—plates that spell names, out-of-state plates
- Items in the bed of a truck—boxes, feed, debris, toolboxes
- Additions to vehicles—luggage rack, bike rack, special lights

Identify the Vehicle Activity

Directions: Draw a line from the description to the vehicle that best matches that description.

A 2-door SUV with a rack on the top and tinted windows in the back
_____

A 4-door SUV with 2-tone colors (light on top and dark on the bottom), a rack on the top, and fog lights
_____

A 2-door sports car with a spoiler on the back and tinted windows
_____

A 4-door truck with a camper shell and tinted windows in the back, and the word SPORT on the side
_____

A 4-door newer model sedan with tinted windows in the back
_____

An older model small-size 4WD truck
_____

Describe the Getaway Car

Directions: Someone just pulled your friend into a car right in front of you. Now it is up to you to describe the getaway car so the police can find the car and your friend. Write down as many details as you can. Refer to the Identifying a Vehicle list to help. Write down at least four details for each car—more if you can. Make up colors to practice remembering the colors of vehicles as well.

1. _____
2. _____
3. _____
4. _____
More: _____
_____

1. _____
2. _____
3. _____
4. _____
More: _____
_____

1. _____
2. _____
3. _____
4. _____
More: _____
_____

More Practice
Parents

Here are some activities you can do with your children to reinforce what they learned in this lesson. You should do this with them regularly to keep their awareness skills sharp. Make it fun.

Randomly pick out a vehicle. Have your child glance at it and quickly turn away. Then have her describe it to you. The more details she gets correct, the more points she can earn. The points can be turned in for whatever reward you choose. The more points she obtains, the better the reward. This can be a fun travel game in the car.

While walking through the store, see how many details your child can give regarding an individual who walks by. Have your child give the person a casual glance. After you have left the store, see how many identifying characteristics your child can remember.

You can also do the same type of activity for the red flags. Remind your child to watch for red flags even if she is with you. Tell her if she spots a red flag to let you know. When she points out a red flag, be sure to say how proud you are of her for being safe and aware.

Lesson 3
Avoidance

Parents

In the previous lesson, your child learned how to identify red flags, or warning signs of potentially dangerous situations. In this lesson, he will learn the next step, how to avoid the danger. In the first part of this lesson, we will review each red flag from lesson 2 and explain what actions your child must take to avoid the potential danger.

In the second part, your child will learn specific ways to deal with strangers who approach her with the *familiarity tactic*. As mentioned in the last lesson, strangers often attempt to trick children into believing they are not a stranger to the child. They do this by using the child's name or talking to the child about something that is familiar, like the baseball team on which the child plays. By talking about something the child is familiar with, the stranger can more easily gain the child's trust. This makes the child more vulnerable to lures and trickery.

Parents can help avoid this tactic from being used on their children by keeping personal information to a minimum when they're in public places. For instance, if a child predator heard a parent say, "Tommy, wait here while Mom goes to the restroom," he might use that information to lure Tommy away. He now knows your child's name and where you went. Read *Tommy and the Sneaky Stranger* within this lesson to see how this information could be used to trick Tommy.

This example also demonstrates another important safety rule. Avoid leaving your children alone without supervision, especially in a public place. Too often adults leave children alone while they go do something, such as pay a bill or use the restroom. This is unsafe. Children can be abducted within seconds. You never think of leaving your wallet or your car keys on a bench outside while you go into the restroom. Remember how precious your children are and keep them with you.

It is important you instruct your child to not take rides from anyone with whom you have not made prior arrangement. Your child should be clear on who is picking him up from school or anywhere. If he is not sure, he may be more easily lured into the car of a child predator. Remember the familiarity tactic. Leaving your child without telling him the exact plan for picking him up puts him at risk.

In case of an emergency, such as if the assigned person cannot pick up your child, you should have a family *code word*. A two-word code such as "purple toad" or "green marshmallow" works best. If for some reason you cannot pick up your child from school and the only person who can help is your coworker who your child does not know, how is your child going to know it is safe to leave with this person? You can tell the coworker the family code word, and she can tell it to your child. This way your child will know you must have sent her.

Make sure you change the code word immediately after you have had to use it. No one else should know the code word except immediate family members. Be careful not to say the code word in public. Remember—strangers are listening. Remind your children that they are not to tell anyone else the code word. Instruct your children not to go with anyone who does not know the code word. Even if that person knows the code word, instruct your children to also check with their teacher or supervising adult, before ever getting into a car with someone they do not know.

The last part of this lesson reviews what to do when your child is home alone. Your child will learn what to say to a stranger who calls on the phone when she is home alone. We will also teach your child what to do if a stranger comes to the door.

Kids

In lesson 2 you learned all about red flags. These are the potentially dangerous situations you see when you are staying aware of what is going on around you. In the first part of this lesson, you are going to learn *what to do* if you see a red flag. You will learn how to avoid the danger and how to avoid the red flags.

In part two of this lesson, you will learn what to do when a stranger tries to play a special trick on you. We call this trick the *familiarity tactic.* You will learn all about how to avoid this type of trick. You will also learn how to properly use the *secret code word.* This will help you identify a safe stranger from an unsafe stranger.

In the third part of this lesson, you will learn what to do when you are home alone. Although it is safer to never be home alone, we know sometimes you will be. In this part of the lesson, you will learn what to say if a stranger calls on the phone or comes to the door.

Learn these important skills, have fun with the activities, and stay safe.

Part One: Avoiding the Red Flags

Avoiding the Common Red Flags

Red flag: Feeling uncomfortable or scared.

If someone ever makes you feel uncomfortable or scared get away from that person immediately. Then go tell your parents or a trusted adult about what happened and how you felt. Do not be afraid to tell someone about your feelings or what happened to you. No one should make you feel uncomfortable or scared.

Red flag: Someone older than you, who you do not know, asks for your help.

Someone older than you, especially an adult, does not need to be asking you for help. Adults and teenagers should get help from people their own age. They should not be asking children for help. Even if the stranger truly needs your help, it is better to be safe and say, "No, I cannot help you." Do not say anything that will make the stranger angry. Just say "no" and walk away.

PLEASE... HELP ME FIND MY LOST DOG.

Red flag: Someone offers you money or gifts.

Unsafe strangers offer things like gifts and money to trick kids into going with them. If a stranger offers you gifts or money, say "no" and walk away. Safe people know you are not being impolite

Red flag: Someone asking to take your picture.

No one is allowed to take your picture unless your parents give permission. Even your school has to get permission from your parents to take your picture. So if someone asks to take your picture, say "no." Tell your parents who was asking to take your picture. Your parents will let you know if it is okay.

Red flag: Someone is trying to touch you in the parts of your body that would be covered by a bathing suit.

The parts of your body covered by a bathing suit are your private areas. No one should be touching those areas of your body, and you should not touch those areas on someone else's body. If *anyone* tries to touch you in these areas or asks you to touch them in their private areas, say "no" or "stop" and get away from them. Tell your parents or a trusted adult right away.

Avoiding Red Flags at Public Places

When you are at a game, the store, a playground, or any large group gathering, avoid the red flags by doing the following:

Red flag: Someone is watching you too long.

If someone, especially an adult, is watching you too long, making you feel uncomfortable, tell a *trusted* adult immediately. If you are with other kids or adults, stay together. Never wander away from your group!

Red flag: An adult who doesn't seem to belong in the area.

If you notice someone who doesn't seem to belong in your area, tell a trusted adult or whoever is supervising you at the time—like your teacher—right away.

Red flag: *Any person you don't know coming toward you.*

If someone you don't know is walking toward you, look to see if there is a reason for him or her to be walking in your direction. Unfortunately, you cannot tell a safe person from an unsafe person just by looking at them. If it seems a person is walking over to you, avoid letting him or her get close to you. Walk away toward a safe place, such as somewhere where there are a lot of people. If a stranger approaches you, keep yourself at least 10 feet away from the stranger at all times. If the stranger calls out to you to come look at something—a puppy, a photograph, a bicycle, a piece of candy, or anything—do not go near the stranger. Tell the stranger "no" and walk away.

Avoiding Red Flags Outside

While walking, playing, or riding your bike outside, avoid the following red flags.

Red flag: Any vehicle that stops along the curb, either in front or behind you, while you are walking along the sidewalk.

Red flag: Anyone getting out of a vehicle and standing next to it in an area near or in the path you must walk.

Red flag: Anyone who gets out of a vehicle and begins to walk toward you.

Red flag: Anyone opening the door of a vehicle near your path.

Red flag: Anyone in a vehicle who appears to be watching you.

Red flag: A vehicle with its motor still running.

Red flag: Anyone leaning against a tree or a wall who is in your path.

You need to keep your distance. Stay at least 10 feet away from the person or vehicle. If you must walk past the person or the vehicle, walk in a half circle around them staying at least 10 feet away. If it is not possible for you to walk around, just cross the street. Keep walking on the opposite side of the street until you feel safe. Stay alert. Watch to make sure the stranger is not trying to follow you. When you are at a stoplight or crosswalk, remember not to get too close to the cars.

Try to always have a friend with you. It is much safer to be with friends than to be alone. If you are playing outside, never leave your yard or play area. Never go into anyone else's house without your parents' permission. Your mom and dad should know where you are at all times. While walking or riding your bike somewhere, do not take shortcuts through alleys or deserted areas. Always go straight to and from your destination.

47

Avoiding Red Flags in Public Bathrooms

When you need to use a public bathroom, avoid the red flags by doing the following.

Red flag: Being alone in the bathroom.

You should never go to a public bathroom alone. Try to always have a trusted adult go with you. If you cannot take a trusted adult into the bathroom with you—for instance, if your mother cannot go into the boys' bathroom— have her wait right outside the bathroom door. When you are in the bathroom, do not waste any time. Use the bathroom, wash your hands, and go back outside.

Red flag: Anyone who was previously sitting or standing nearby who now walks toward the bathroom when you walk to the bathroom.

If someone you do not know seems to be following you, especially to a less crowded place like the bathroom, wait for the person to leave or use another bathroom. *Do not go into the bathroom alone.* Tell the adult with you that you are concerned someone is following you.

🚩 *Red flag:* Anyone you don't know trying to talk to you in the bathroom.

It is not safe to talk to someone you do not know in the bathroom. If someone does try to talk to you there, tell them you must leave and then walk out. Leave the bathroom right then. You can finish your business in another bathroom or wait for that person to leave before you go back in. Don't forget to tell the adult with you someone tried to talk to you in the bathroom and that is the reason you left without finishing. The adult will understand and be happy you chose to be safe.

49

Avoiding Red Flags While in the Car

When you are in the car with an adult, avoid red flags by doing the following.

Red flag: Someone in the car parked next to you gives you a bad feeling or worries you.

Anytime you have a bad feeling or something worries you, tell the adult who is with you.

Red flag: Someone is following you in another vehicle.

If you suspect someone is following you in another vehicle, tell the driver of the car you are in right away.

Red flag: Being told to wait in the car alone.

You should never wait alone in a car. Remind the person with you to be safe and not leave you alone or even with other kids. There must be a responsible teenager or adult with you if you are to wait in the car.

Red flag: Parking in a dark area.

Staying in a lighted area is safer. People and lights sometimes discourage unsafe people from coming around. Remind the person you are with to park in an area with lots of light, if possible, rather than a dark area.

Red flag: Someone in another vehicle is looking at you or anyone in the car with you too long.

If someone is staring at you too long, do not stare back at the person. Tell the driver of the car you are in what you see.

Part Two: Avoiding the Familiarity Tactic

Kids

Sometimes a stranger—someone you do not know well—may try to trick you into thinking he or she is not a stranger. This person may call you by your name or talk to you about a sports team on which you play. This is a trick an unsafe stranger may use. We call it the *familiarity tactic* because his or her plan (tactic) is to trick you into thinking this person is someone you know (are familiar with). Don't fall for these tricks. Don't let the stranger fool you. Unless you know someone really well, you should not talk to him or her when you are alone or even if you're with other kids. Even if you know the person a little (like the guy next door), be safe and do not talk to someone you do not know very well. It is only okay when your parents or a supervising adult are with you.

Tommy and the Sneaky Stranger

Directions: Act out the following scenario about Tommy and the Sneaky Stranger. You'll need three actors; try to get mom and dad to do it with you. After you act out the scenario, discuss how the stranger used the familiarity tactic to lure Tommy away.

Mom: "Tommy, you stay right here while I go use the bathroom."(Mom walks down to the bathroom. A stranger walks up to Tommy.)

Stranger: "Hi, Tommy. How are you? I saw you looking at that toy airplane over by the front entrance. That is a really neat airplane."

Tommy: "Yeah, I thought so too. Who are you? I am not supposed to talk to strangers."

Stranger: "I'm no stranger, Tommy. I work in the camping department. Remember last year I helped you and your mom pick out a sleeping bag for your Boy Scout trip?"

Tommy: "Oh yeah, I think I remember you now."

Stranger: "Hey, your mom saw me when she was walking to the bathroom and told me it was okay to take you over to look at that airplane again. What do you say? Do you want to have another look at it? I think she was thinking about getting it for you."

Tommy: "Well, if my mom said it was okay, I guess I can."

(Tommy leaves with the stranger toward the front entrance. A few minutes later, Tommy's mom returns.)

Mom: "Tommy, where are you?"

What's in a Name?

Directions: Write down the names of the following common things a stranger might use to try to sound like he or she knows you. Fill in as many of the blanks as you can. If you can't fill in some of them—such as if you don't play on a sports team—don't worry about it.

Your name _____

Your friends' names _____

Your parents' names _____

Name of your school _____

Name of sports teams you've been on _____

Name of the street(s) you live on _____

Name of the church you go to _____

Name of any clubs you belong to (such as the Boy Scouts)_____

_____

Name of hobbies you enjoy (such as drawing) _____

Remember that these names can be used to trick you. Lots of people may know this information about you. A stranger can find out what sports team you play on or what team you like by noticing the name on your shirt or hat. He or she might have seen you around at a movie, game, or just walking home from the bus stop. He or she may have overheard your mom or dad call out your name or say something about you. Just because someone knows something about you does not mean the person is safe. If you do not know the person well, even if he or she seems to know things about you, that person is still a stranger. And since we cannot tell safe strangers from unsafe strangers, you must stay away. Do not fall for tricks like the familiarity tactic.

The Secret Code

Normally you should never get into the car or go anywhere with someone you have not already gotten permission from your parents to go with. Your parents should always tell you who will be picking you up from school or practice, or anywhere. However, what if there was an emergency and the person who was supposed to pick you up couldn't come? If this were to happen, your parents should try to get a message to you somehow that the plans have changed.

If your parents can't get a message to you, you may have to rely on a code word. Sometimes a stranger (like your mom's friend from work) may have to pick you up. In this case, the person should know the code word. Your mom or dad would tell them the code word, so the person can tell you. If a stranger tells you that your mom or dad sent him or her, remember to keep your distance and ask, "What's the secret code"? If this person knows the secret code, go tell a supervising adult—such as your teacher or coach—that a stranger is here to pick you up. Ask the supervising adult to please talk with the stranger to make sure it is okay for you to go with him or her. If the stranger is a police officer and does not know the secret code, you must also check with your teacher or a supervising adult to verify the person is who they say they are.

After you have used the code, you and your parents must change it. The only people who should know the secret code are those in your immediate family. Do not tell anyone the code or say it in public! Remember, the secret code is only for emergencies. The general rule is you never get in the car or go anywhere with someone you do not know. You and your parents may already have decided on your secret code. If you already have a code, write it down on the lines below. There are two lines because it is best if your code is two words, such as purple toad.

If you don't already have a code, make one up right now. Talk to your parents and write your secret code down below. Write the code down twice. After you have written your secret code both times, cut them out on the dotted lines. Keep one for yourself. Store it in a safe place, like your desk at home. Then give the second copy to your mom or dad. Tell them to keep the code in a safe place where they could find it if they needed to. Remind them that they should not use the secret code unless it is an emergency and only close family should know what it is.

Secret Code Words

_____   _____

_____   _____

Part Three: Home Alone

Kids

The Mysterious Phone Call

Another way a stranger may try to get information is by calling on the phone. He or she may try to find out if you are alone or where you live. You should never give out any information over the phone.

Act out the following phone call. You need two actors for this one. Take note of all the information Susan should *not* have said to the stranger on the phone.

(The phone rings.)

Susan: "Hello."

Stranger: "Hi, this is Frank. I work with your dad. Can I talk to him?"

Susan: "He is not home right now."

Stranger: "Oh no! I have some things he asked for. I told him I would drop them off to him today, but I lost the address he gave me."

Susan: "I'm sorry, but he is not home."

Stranger: "That's okay. How about your mom? Can I talk to her?"

Susan: "She's not home either."

Stranger: "Uh-oh! That's not good. Your dad will not be happy if I can't get this stuff to him today. I need to drop this stuff off."

Susan: "I can have him call you when he gets home."

Stranger: "When will he get home?"

Susan: "At about six o'clock tonight."

Stranger: "Okay. I will stop by after six tonight. By the way, what did you say your name was?"

Susan: "Susan."

Stranger: "Thanks, Susan. Oh, I almost forgot, can I get your address again?"

Susan: "Sure, it is Smith Lane. Just look for the house with the boat in the driveway."

Stranger: "Thanks again, Susan, you've been a great help. See you soon."

Did you note how many times Susan gave out information she shouldn't have? She told a stranger information that put her in danger. Can you name some of the things Susan told the stranger that she shouldn't have?

1. _____

2. _____

3. _____

4. _____

5. _____

How would you have answered that phone call?

Susan should have said, "I am sorry, but my father is busy right now. Can I take a message?" That is all she should have said, nothing more. If the stranger tried to ask questions, she should just have kept repeating that line.

Follow the phone safety rules:

● Never give out information over the telephone to strangers.

● Never tell a stranger you are home alone.

● Never tell a stranger your name.

● Never tell a stranger where you live.

● Memorize this line for answering the phone:

"I am sorry, my _____ (mom, dad, whoever) is busy right now. Can I take a message?"

Practice it. Memorize it. This is all you should say to people on the phone when your parents are not home.

A Stranger at the Door

Although it is best if you aren't at home alone, sometimes you will be. When you are home alone, follow these simple safety rules:

● Always keep all the doors to the outside locked.

● If someone comes to the door, try to see who it is without letting the person outside see you. Look through a peephole or out a nearby window. Unless you know the person and were expecting him or her to come over, do not open the door or try to talk to the person through the door. If the person leaves, there is no problem.

● If someone is trying to get into the house, call 911 immediately.

● Make sure there is an emergency phone list near the phone.

Emergency Phone List

With your parents' help, fill out the phone list below. Then cut it out on the dotted line and put it by the phone. You need to make sure the phone numbers are checked and updated every time you will be alone.

Emergency numbers: 911 or O

Parents' work numbers: _____

_____

Parents' cell phone numbers: _____

Name and phone number of the nearest relative:

_____

Name and phone number of the nearest friend or neighbor:

_____

Our address: _____

Our phone number: _____

Other important numbers for the sitter or your parents:

_____

_____

_____

Doctor's name and phone number: _____

Poison Control Center phone number: _____

Lesson 4
Escape

Parents

There is only one objective to this lesson: to teach your child how to escape from an attack. Even if your child identifies a red flag and takes the necessary precautions to avoid it, she may still find herself at the point of an attack. The child predator may follow her, chase her, or catch her off guard. Thus, your child needs to know how to react if she comes in close contact with an attacker. The self-defense techniques taught in this lesson are very basic. They are practical and effective for children and adults alike. The basic premise is to distract the attacker, yell, and run. The objective is to avoid being grabbed.

Please note that we do not attempt to teach the children how to escape once they have been grabbed or how to fight an attacker. If you wish your children to take their self-defense knowledge a step further, enroll them in children's self-defense courses. When it comes to truly having to fight an adult, your child needs to have hands-on training from professionals. Learning to effectively defend yourself once you are physically being attacked takes skill and advanced instruction.

Your child will need your help with this lesson. You will need to pose as the attacker by trying to grab her and chase her. This will help her practice the techniques and build her confidence. Oh, and don't worry, the sand in your eyes will come out with lots of water. No, we are just kidding. You don't have to go as far as letting your child throw sand in your eyes, but let her practice her techniques as close to reality as possible. Take her outside and let her run around while you chase her. Let her yell. And make sure you warn the neighbors you're just practicing your child's safety skills.

Kids

So far you have learned how to recognize a dangerous situation (a red flag) and how to avoid it. Now we are going to take you to the next level of danger. What if you didn't notice the red flag, or the danger sign? Or what if you noticed the red flag and took the proper steps to avoid it, but the danger remained? What if the unsafe person was now following you, chasing you, or trying to grab you?

In this lesson, you will learn how to avoid being grabbed. You will learn how to distract an attacker and get out of danger. You will need an adult to do this lesson.

Throwing Things in the Eyes

If you notice a red flag, it is always a good idea to be ready in case it turns into a real attack. One of the ways to be ready is to put something in your hand you can use to temporarily block the attacker's vision. If you are unable to avoid the person and he or she reaches out to grab you, throw the object hard in the person's face. Throw it in her eyes or as close to the eyes as you can. Scream loudly while you throw the object. You can yell, "No, leave me alone!" or "Help, he (or she) is trying to hurt me!" or "You're not my mother!" or "Get away from me!"—anything that may warn people around that you are being attacked. Then run as fast as you can to a safe place or safe person. Keep screaming as you run.

Directions: Look at this picture. How many things do you see that you can use to help you escape?

Name some other things that you can use:

_____

_____

_____

Distracting the Attacker

If an unsafe person gets too close to you or tries to grab you, you can try to distract him by throwing things in his or her eyes, but you can also use larger objects to distract or trip the person so you can run.

Directions: Read the following things you can do to protect yourself. Then practice these techniques with your parent(s).

● If you are carrying a backpack, slide it off to one shoulder. As the person grabs for you, throw the pack at the person's feet, drop low, and run. Don't forget to yell loudly.

● You can also swing your backpack, jacket, lunch box, gear bag, or any object that is near you to block the attacker's hands. As he or she reaches out to grab you, swing the object around in a circular motion to hit the person's hands. Then run.

● Or you can use these large objects to avoid escape by throwing them hard at the person's face.

● If you are walking with or riding your bike and someone tries to grab you, drop your bike right at their feet and run. The bike will give the person an obstacle to have to get over before he or she can come after you. If you can get away on your bike, however, that is even better. Only drop your bike at the person's feet if you know you need a distraction fast, and you cannot ride away. Just like when you're walking, when riding your bike try to avoid strangers by riding at least 10 feet away.

The Box Run

Running away from an attacker takes more than just moving your legs fast. If the attacker decides to chase you, you will need to know *how to run* to keep out of his or her reach. If you were to run straight, the attacker may be able to catch you. The box run is one way you can run to avoid being grabbed. Use this type of run if you are in an enclosed area, such as a room, while you are trying to get to an exit.

Directions: You will need an adult to help you learn this technique. Corner off an area of at least 12 by 12 feet. You should have four defined corners and an exit. Both you and the adult must get into the "box." The adult must stand at least 5 feet from you. Tell the adult to clap, then try to grab you.

As soon as you hear the clap, start running. Run to any corner. After you reach the corner, turn as quickly as you can and run to the next corner until you reach your exit. Usually the adult will not be able to catch you. The adult must chase you around the corners and not cut across to grab you. Don't be discouraged if the adult catches you sometimes. Make sure you change the corner you first run to, so that the adult doesn't figure out where to start. In real life, the attacker will not know which way you are going to run or that you are running in a box to get to the exit. Practice this several times until you know the technique well.

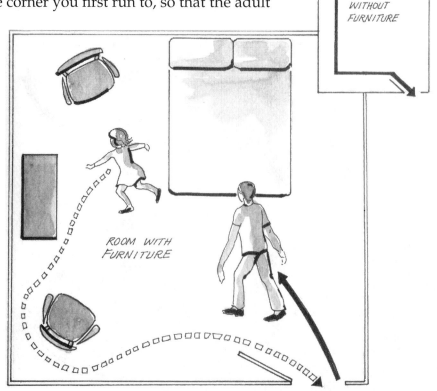

ROOM WITHOUT FURNITURE

ROOM WITH FURNITURE

Cut and Run

Directions: This technique is great for when you are outside or in a wider area. The idea is to be able to make quick movements (cuts) one direction or another to avoid being grabbed. It is also great for running around or in between objects to escape an attacker. When in danger, you can *run around corners* of buildings, vehicles, bushes, fences, or trees. You can also *cut between objects*, especially those too close for an adult to pass through. You can run between two parked cars, rows of boxes, or openings in fences. You can even *cut under objects* as well as going through small openings that an adult cannot crawl through. You can go under fences, debris, guardrails, or handrails. And don't forget to yell. Have one of your parents chase you around while you try to cut around, in between, and under objects to get away.

The Zigzag

Directions: This is the *box run* and *cut and run* techniques put together. Once again you will need your parents or another adult to help you. First, you will need to set up an obstacle course in a large area that has definite corners, such as a fenced backyard. Place chairs randomly within the area. Then lay bags, pillows, or pads at various spots between the chairs. Finally, balance things on some of the objects, such as a broom on two chairs. Once you are set up, have the adult start to chase you. As the adult tries to grab you, run in a zigzag between the objects. Practice jumping, dropping, rolling, and crawling around the objects to keep from being grabbed. Make quick movements; don't stop and think about what you are going to do. When you are at the corners of the area turn as in the box run. The more you practice all these techniques, the better your chances of getting away. You will naturally know how to run and avoid being grabbed.

Lesson 5
Where to Find Help

Sir, can you help me call my mom?

Parents

After your child has escaped an attack, he will need to find help. He will need to know where to go and who to turn to. In this lesson, your child will learn how to get help when he is away from home.

First, we will explain how to identify a low-risk versus a high-risk adult. As we stated before, some strangers are safe and some are dangerous, and we cannot identify which type of stranger they are by just looking at them. We can, however, identify a person who is less likely to be dangerous, a low-risk adult, and someone who is more likely to be dangerous, a high-risk adult. Your child will also learn the most likely places to find a low-risk adult.

Once your child has found someone to help him, he will need to be able to tell that person who he is and how to get in contact with you. It is important you provide your child with an identification card. This card should include the child's name, address, home phone number, and other phone and pager numbers that can be used to reach you. One of the activities in this lesson will include filling out an identification card your child can cut out and keep with him.

Another important item your child should carry is enough change to make a few phone calls. Your child may need to use a pay phone to call you. Suppose your daughter was to be taken home by her friend's mom after dance practice, but her friend didn't come to practice that day. She could use the money to call you and let you know she needed a ride home. Your child will also learn that if she does not have money for the pay phone, she could call the operator and inform the operator she needs help making a phone call. She could also call 911 if it is an emergency. Providing a cell phone for your child is another great option for your child to communicate with you.

Kids

In the last lesson, you learned how to escape when someone is trying to grab you. You learned not only should you yell, you should run. Do you know where to run? Should you run home? That would be correct if home is the closest safe place and there was someone there. But what if home was too far or no one was at home? Home might not always be the best place to run for help if you are in danger. In this lesson, you will learn the best places to run to. You will also learn who to run to and what to tell them.

The Safe House

In the last lesson, you learned that if someone tries to grab you, you must run to a safe place or safe person. Always run to the *closest* safe place or safe person. If your home is the closest safe place and someone is at home, *run home*.

If you are not near your home or there is no one at home, the next best person to turn to is *someone you know* who is close by. It is a good idea for you and your parents to make a plan in case of an emergency like this. You and your parents should identify people you can go to for help if your parents are not around. This may be a relative, neighbor, or friend. Identify several people in different places you may be without supervision, such as a ballpark, playground, or the route you walk home from school.

Directions: Fill in the spaces below to identify places you would go to for help if you were in danger or frightened. After completing this activity, if you are ever being followed, or bullied, or get hurt, you will know some safe places to find help.

● If I need help when I am walking home from school, I could go to

_____

● If a stranger is trying to talk to me at the park, I could run to

_____

● If an older kid tried to bully me on the way to my friend's house, I could go to_____

● If I am in danger, but near my home and someone is at home, I should _____

● If I am being followed near my home, but no one is at home, I would go to _____

Can you think of any more places where you may need to find help fast? With your parents' help, list any additional safe places (where there are people you know) that you can go to.

_____

_____

_____

Low-Risk or High-Risk Stranger?

You learned in the first lesson that you cannot tell if someone is unsafe or safe by just looking at him or her. Normally, you should stay away from people you do not know, but there are times when you must go to a stranger for help. If you are not near someplace or someone you and your parents have identified to be safe, you will have to turn to a stranger.

Even though you cannot tell if someone is unsafe or safe by just looking at him or her, you can tell who is less likely or more likely to be dangerous. A stranger who is more likely to be dangerous is called a *high-risk adult.* An example of a high-risk adult is a man who is alone in an isolated area. A *low-risk adult* is someone who is less likely to be dangerous to you. If you are frightened, hurt, lost, or in danger, you can turn to a low-risk adult for help.

Here are some examples of low-risk adults or places you can find them:

● *At school*—teacher, yard monitor, bus driver, office workers, principal, janitor, cafeteria workers.

● *While shopping in a public place*—security personnel, store clerks, help desks, lost-and-found desks, and checkout stands are all places you could turn to for help (look for someone with a name tag, apron, or some other clothing that might identify them as an employee). A pregnant woman or a woman with other children is a low-risk adult as well.

● *While outside:* You could run to a police station, fire station, a medical building such as a hospital, post office, bank, store, or any other building with lots of people inside.

● *Anywhere*—police officers, firemen, paramedics, medical personnel, forest rangers, or people wearing a uniform are often low-risk strangers to whom you can turn.

Remember it is always safer to approach strangers in an area with lots of people around. So if you need help, try to first go to an area with lots of people, then search for a low-risk adult.

The Stranger

Directions: Circle the low-risk strangers (less likely to be dangerous) and put an X over the high-risk strangers (more likely to be dangerous).

Risky Puzzle

Directions: In the word puzzle below, find all the low-risk people or places and things that may help you find low-risk people.

Find these words:

- policeman
- fireman
- paramedic
- store
- bank
- hospital
- uniform
- name tag
- woman
- security
- help desk
- apron
- crowded area
- ranger
- post office
- teacher
- bus driver
- yard monitor
- principal
- office

```
L A E K E O S N G T E A C H E R T R B Y P D F
O I P Q U P E R Y T N K S V O L Q P Z A I V R
M J G R C L C N U N I F O R M X A R S T N O C
P E Z N O I U T M E V Q F J O M W I T N S K B
K R A G U N R P M N I U V T Y C E N W A Z Q F
R A N G E R I U H O S P I T A L N C X M P O I
E T A P O S T O F F I C E O R V N I V E F A R
Z S O A S D Y F G H J K H N D A R P U T P O E
N B U R W E R T Y U I P E O M B V A C A X I M
S N B U S D R I V E R A L I O E O L P G B F A
U T Y T R E W B N M I G P H N V F Y W E R T N
K P O P O L I C E M A N D T I G F D P B T C E
L D S R O W F E D R R M E W T L I F W O M A N
A B R N E W V Q C E M Y S U O P C P R A A T S
S T R A N G W O V M A P K U R R E C R O W D E
P A R A M E D I C O B N C R O W D E D A R E A
```

Using a Pay Phone

Using a pay phone may be a smart thing to do as well. You may need to call your parents or another trusted adult if you need a ride, are frightened, or are in danger. In order to use a pay phone you need money. The cost of the call depends on how far the person you are calling lives. You should carry at least $1 in change to make a call. One call usually costs less than this, but you may have to make a few calls.

If you need to use the pay phone but do not have any money, you can dial "O" for the operator. The operator can help you make a phone call in an emergency, without money. Make sure you explain the situation to the operator. The operator may feel it is necessary to call the police to help you.

If you are in danger, you should call the emergency number 911. If you call 911, whether from your own home or a pay phone, the person who answers the 911 call automatically can tell where the call is coming from. Even if you just dial 911 and hang up before it rings, the address of the phone you are calling from is displayed for the 911 operator. They will send someone out to help you at that location. So even if you called on a pay phone and didn't know where you were or how to tell them where you were, they will find you.

Remember that calling "O" for the operator or "911" for the police is free.

The rule here is to make sure when you go to use a pay phone, you are safe from any danger. If someone tried to grab you or make you go somewhere with him or her, you must be sure you are safely away from that person. Only use a phone booth located in a place where there are lots of people around. It may be safer for you to approach a low-risk adult to ask for help if you feel you are in any danger. You can even call 911, then approach a low-risk adult to stay with you until the police arrive.

If you have a cell phone, you can use it to call 911 in an emergency. The 911 operator will know the cell phone number you are using, but he or she will not know where you are. You must be able to tell the operator where you are. It is best if you can tell the operator an exact address, but you can also tell him or her street names, names of buildings and stores, or any other specific information about your location that may help the police find you.

Identify Yourself

When you turn to strangers for help, you must be able to tell them enough about you to enable them to help you. First, tell the stranger what is wrong. Tell the person if you are in danger, frightened, or hurt. Then tell them who you are. In order to do this, you must have information about yourself and your family so the stranger can contact your family.

It is smart to memorize all this information, but when you are scared or hurt you may not be able to remember it. It is best to have the information written down on a card. This information should be kept with you at all times. It is much safer to keep it in a place such as your pocket than in your backpack. If you had to drop your backpack to defend yourself, you would not want the attacker to get your personal identification. Talk to your parents about the best places to put your identification card. It will likely depend on what you're doing and where you are.

Directions: Ask your parents to help you fill out all the information below. Then copy the information to the card at the back of the book (look on the inside portion of the back cover). After you complete the book, cut out this information card and keep it with you at all times.

You should memorize this information. If you lose your card for any reason (such as it was in the backpack you just threw at an attacker), you will need to be able to tell the person helping you the information from memory. After you have filled in the blanks, practice making the calls. Call the numbers to be sure you know how.

● Your full name (first, middle, and last) _____

● Your mom's full name _____

● Your dad's full name _____

● Stepparents' full names (if any) _____

● Your home phone number _____

● Your parents' cell phone number(s) _____

● Your parents' pager number(s) _____

● Your parents' work number(s) _____

● Your parents' place(s) of work _____

● Phone number of a close relative or friend _____

● Your home address, including city and state _____

_____

● Landmarks near your home (such as by "the yellow church." This may help you or a stranger locate your home more easily.)

_____

Lesson 6

But What If?

Parents

What if the unsafe person is not a stranger? What if the unsafe person is someone your child knows and trusts? This is, unfortunately, often the case. According to the Department of Justice, 90 percent of child rape victims under the age of 12 knew their offender. How can you keep your child from becoming the victim of an acquaintance child molester? What if the offender is a family member? In this lesson, *you* will learn the danger signs to watch for to help avoid or detect the sexual abuse of your child. We also have included tips on how to keep the communication line open with your child. In this lesson, your child will learn the "red flags" to watch for around people they know and what to do if someone they know tries to hurt them.

Acquaintance child molesters use seduction and coercion to control and abuse children. Unfortunately, they are very skilled at what they do. They often seek out jobs where they can gain access to children. They are often considered the "nice guy." Once they are in a position to be around children, they work to gain not only the trust of the child, but the trust of the child's parents. The child molester's home is often filled with games, toys, and equipment that appeals to the age group the molester prefers. They seduce the child with gifts, affection, or attention. They gradually work to lower the sexual inhibitions of the child. It may start as a conversation about sex. It may then progress to looking at pictures of naked people and staging fondling games. Then before your child even realizes it, she has become a victim of sexual abuse.

The offender continues the abuse by controlling the child through blackmail, threats, or increased seduction. The child may be too ashamed, confused, or afraid to tell anyone. She may not even understand that what has happened to her is wrong. Children's needs for attention and affection, their natural curiosity, and their naivety make them ideal victims. Furthermore, children are often victimized by other children or adolescents. The abuser could be a favorite cousin or a best friend's older brother she happens to really like.

So what can you do? You can start by finding out as much as you can about anybody who comes in regular contact with your child. Many states allow you to access information about sex offenders in your area. Take the time to be sure the people your children spend time with are safe, especially if they are to be alone with them. Check references on the babysitter you are considering. If your child is going to be in an after-school program or daycare, ensure the program or the center is reputable. You can obtain information about these places from the State Department of Social Services, Community Care Licensing Division, childcare information or referral services, or other childcare community agencies. Prohibit anyone from taking your child off the premises without your written permission. Drop in and visit unexpectedly to check on your child.

When your child attends after-school activities, try to be there too. Your presence will not only enable you to monitor the interaction between your child and other adults, but may also deter potential child predators from selecting your child as a potential target because of your attentiveness. Furthermore, pay attention to your own feelings. If someone concerns you or makes you feel uncomfortable, trust yourself and keep your child away from that person.

If parents had shown a lot more interest in their children, my activities with them would have been very much more difficult.
—a convicted child molester, *Child Molesters Who Abduct: Summary of the Case in Point Series*

What Parents Should Be Watching For

Always pay attention to the interaction between your children and those around them, whether they are with family, friends, or strangers. That doesn't mean you have to be paranoid; you just need to pay attention to your children's safety in regard to sexual predators much as you would be alert to the dangers around them while they are swimming at the beach. If you notice any of the following danger signs, pay close attention to the people with whom your child is spending time.

Watch for these *danger signs* among those who interact with your child:
- Someone who shows more interest in one child than another.
- Someone who always finds a way to be alone with your child for a period of time.
- Someone who seems to find ways to touch the child more than normal.
- Someone who has the child sit very close (especially on his or her lap) for long periods of time.
- Someone who involves the child in tickling or touching games.
- Someone who seems to watch your child more than normal, especially when other events are going on that would normally capture his or her attention.
- Someone who brings too many gifts or inappropriate gifts to your child or one child more than another.

Sometimes your child may show *physical signs* that some type of abuse may be occurring. Watch for the following physical signs:
- The child may complain of loss of appetite, stomachaches, or headaches.
- He may walk differently or seem uncomfortable sitting down.
- She may have torn or stained underclothing.
- He may also have more blatant signs, such as venereal disease or injuries to the genitals or other parts of the body.

Sometimes your child may show *emotional or social signs* that some type of abuse may be occurring. Watch for the following emotional or social signs:
- She may have a sudden decrease in school performance.
- He may not interact well with other children.
- She may be unwilling to undress in front of others.
- He may become depressed, apathetic, or suicidal.
- She may have recurrent nightmares or disturbed sleep patterns.
- He may become withdrawn or fearful, or cry without any obvious reason.
- She may have sexual knowledge or interest beyond her age.
- He may regress to things he did as a younger child, such as thumb sucking or bed wetting.
- She may act differently around a particular person, such as refusing to be alone with or showing intense dislike for this person. She may also ask to be alone with this person more often.
- He may develop delinquent behavior or try to run away.

Parents, Let's Talk

Educating your children about sexual abuse, paying attention to their needs and interests, and maintaining good open communication with them are the most important things you can do to protect them from child predators. Here are some tips and ideas to help you stay close to and communicate well with your children:

- Set aside some special time at least once a week where you and your child can be together. It can be something as simple as going for a walk or a bike ride.

- Eat meals together as often as possible and encourage open discussions during meals. During dinner, one great way to encourage your family to talk with each other is to have everyone answer this question: What was the worst thing and the best thing that happened to you today?

- Learn about your child's interests. Then try to learn about those things and show interest in them as well.

- Tell your children what you think and ask them what they think about different issues.

- Set limits and make sure your children know the rules, such as not going anywhere without permission. Remind them that you make the rules because you care about their safety.

- Talk to your children about different types of touching. I highly recommend you read Jan Hindman's *A Very Touching Book* (Alexandria Assoc., 1983). This book is a wonderful tool for explaining appropriate and inappropriate types of touching to children.

- Encourage your children to talk to you about anything that concerns them.

- Listen attentively. Repeat back to them what they tell you, so they know you are listening.

- Listen to their point of view, even if it is difficult to hear. Do not interrupt them.

- Respond calmly when your child says something that disturbs you. Children will tune you out if you seem angry. They may also choose not to tell you anything else that may disturb you.

- Do not belittle your child's thoughts, opinions, or ideas. Tell your child what you think without putting her down.

- Be specific when you praise your child. Tell him exactly what he did that was good.

- And finally, if your child tells you she has been abused, believe her. Children rarely lie about sexual abuse.

Kids

So far you have learned what to do if a stranger comes too close to you, tries to trick you or grab you. However, what if the person trying to hurt you was not a stranger? What if the unsafe person was a friend or someone in your family? Sometimes it is hard to understand that someone you care about or trust may try to hurt you. Some people who at first seem very nice can actually be unsafe. This does not mean you should be afraid of nice friends or family members. Most adults care about children and would never try to hurt you. But you need to be aware of things to watch out for, just in case someone you know tries to hurt you.

Just like the red flags you learned before, in this lesson you will learn what red flags to watch for with people you know. You will also learn what to do if someone you know tries to hurt you or does hurt you.

Red Flags With People You Know

Watch for the following red flags even at home with people you know:

Red flag: Someone makes you feel uncomfortable or scared for any reason.

Pay attention to your feelings. If you feel uncomfortable or afraid, this is a warning something may be wrong. Trust yourself. Get away from whoever or whatever is making you feel this way. Don't forget to tell an adult you trust, such as your parents, about how you felt and what made you feel that way.

Red flag: Someone staring at you too much, making you uncomfortable.

Sometimes it is okay when people are looking at you for a long time, such as when you are doing something you want them to see—like showing your grandpa how good of a swimmer you are. Other times someone may be staring at you when you do not want him or her to. If someone is staring at you and making you feel uncomfortable, tell your mom, dad, or another trusted adult right away.

Red flag: Someone who tries to be alone with you a lot without anyone else around or asks that you meet him or her somewhere, but tells you not to tell anyone—even your parents.

Unsafe people like to get kids in places where there are no other people around. You should never go anywhere without your parents' permission.

Red flag: Someone is touching you too much.

Some touching is okay, such as shaking hands with your coach or giving your aunt a hug. But too much touching may make you uncomfortable and may be a red flag. Talk to your mom and dad about the different types of touching. Remember to trust your feelings. If someone is touching you too much or too long, or in ways you don't like, tell him or her to stop. Do not be afraid of being rude or impolite. It is much better to be safe and protect yourself. Remember—safe people will understand.

What-If Game

Directions: Read and discuss the scenarios below with your parents. None of these scenarios is necessarily bad. This is just an exercise to enable you to think about different situations that might make you uncomfortable and what you would do if they occurred.

- What if your teacher asked you to stay alone with him during recess? What would you do?

- What if your aunt started to rub your arm and you felt uncomfortable? What would you do?

- What if your friend's brother asked you to come sleep in his room? What would you do?

- What if your coach patted your behind? What would you do?

- What if the babysitter asked you to rub her back? What would you do?

- What if your uncle walked into the bedroom when you were changing your clothes? What would you do?

Kids, Let's Talk

If anyone makes you uncomfortable or tries to hurt you, or if you notice any of the red flags, you should always tell a trusted adult. In most cases, the first person you talk to will help you. But if you ever tell someone one of these things and he or she does not help you, tell someone else. Do not give up. If an unsafe person is hurting you or making you uncomfortable, keep telling adults you know and trust until you get help.

Directions: Write down the names of some adults you know and trust and draw a picture of them above his or her name.

1. _____

2. _____

3. _____

4. _____

5, _____

6, _____

Lesson 7
Staying Safe in Cyberspace

Parents

Children all over the world use the Internet to obtain information, talk with people, or play games. The Internet is a wonderful way to learn about anything and everything. Chat rooms, where you talk with someone or a group of people via the Internet, have become very popular. Although the Internet is good for many wonderful things, it has also become a new way for predators to victimize children.

One of the risks of using the Internet is your child being exposed to unwanted sexual material. One in four children who use the Internet regularly are exposed to pictures of naked people or people having sex. Another risk is that your child will be sexually solicited online. One in five children who uses the Internet regularly receives a sexual solicitation or approach over the Internet.

Interaction with strangers online can even lead to physical molestation. Sometimes children may purposely or inadvertently provide information to a stranger. The stranger may use the information to find the child. Some children even agree to meet someone they have corresponded with on the Internet, without the parents' permission or knowledge. This exposes the child to potential physical molestation, exploitation, and abduction.

Unfortunately, many parents are not even aware of what their children are being exposed to. In one study, only about 25 percent of the youths who were sexually solicited told a parent. And only 40 percent of youths who were exposed to unwanted sexual material told a parent. Even when the parents were aware of the problem, a great majority of them did not know to whom to report such an incident. Only 10 percent of parents could name a specific authority to which they could make a report.

In this lesson, your children will learn how to stay safe on the Internet. They will learn how to avoid places on the Internet that expose them to sexually explicit material. They will also learn how to avoid the tactics of child predators and other dangerous people online. At the end of the lesson, your child will complete a set of rules to keep by the computer all the time. This will help him remember how to stay safe.

Even if you do not have a computer at home, this is an important lesson. The Internet is everywhere. Your child can log on at school, the library, a friend's house, or even in a cyber café.

One of the activities within this lesson requires Internet access. If you do not have Internet access at home, please give your child the opportunity to complete the lesson somewhere, such as a library, so she can learn how to avoid danger.

Although your child will know a great deal more about staying safe on the Internet after the lesson, there is still some risk. Parents, please regularly monitor your child's Internet use. You should also use an Internet filter, which can greatly decrease your child's risk. We have included an activity that will teach your child about Internet filters. These can help keep unwanted material from coming into your home or a family member inadvertently coming across unwanted material.

If your child does come across some unwanted material or is solicited or harassed, do not blame him. Just report the incident to the authorities and review the Internet safety rules with him. For more information on Internet safety or how to report an incident, refer to the resources page toward the end of the book.

(Statistics in this section were obtained from *Online Victimization: A Report on the Nation's Youth*, published by the National Center for Missing and Exploited Children. This report was based on a study of children ages 10 to 17, who used the Internet at least once a month.)

Kids

So far you have learned how to stay safe while outside, at school, at home, and everywhere else you like to go. But what about the Internet? Millions of kids all over the world use the internet to get information, talk to each other, or just play games. The Internet is a great place to learn about almost anything you want to know about. But the Internet can also be used by unsafe people. Some unsafe people use the Internet to reach kids.

Getting on the Internet, without knowing how to stay safe, can be as dangerous as opening the front door when an unsafe person is knocking outside. It is very important that you and your family learn to be safe when using the internet. In this lesson, you will learn how to stay safe in cyberspace.

Let's Go Online

Since you are learning to be safe on the Internet, let's go online. To complete this activity, follow the directions below. It will probably take you a few sessions to complete all the activities on the website. Take your time and have fun.

Directions: Go to the www.NetSmartz.org website on the Internet. Click on NetSmartz kids. You may need to first download the Flash™ plug-in, which is required. Complete all of the activities, and check them off after you have completed them.

● *Clicky's Web World*

____ What 2 Do on the Web

____ The Webville Outlaws

____ Clicky's Challenge

● For more Internet fun, you can play the games in Clicky's Web World or NetSmartz Rules.

● *NetSmartz Rules*

____ NetSmartz What to Do on the Web

____ Meet the Wizzywigs

____ Wizzywig Guessing Game 1

____ Who's Your Friend on the Internet?

____ Wizzywig Guessing Game 2

____ Protect Your Personal Information

____ Which Wizzywig is Which?

Filters

There are different ways the Internet can be filtered. By this we mean you are kept from seeing unsafe things and talking to unsafe people on the Internet, and they are kept from being able to get to you on your computer. To use the Internet you must have an Internet service provider (ISP). The ISP is what makes the connection between you and all the other computers connected to the Internet. Through your ISP you can send or receive mail from your friends or family, get into a chat room and talk with other kids about things that interest you, or get information for a school project. Many ISPs provide a filtering system for families to keep out unsafe things.

Directions: Answer the questions below to help your family stay safe on the Internet:

- What is the name of the ISP your family uses for your home computer?

- Does the ISP your family uses have a filtering program? If yes, what is the name of it? (You can look on your ISP home page—usually this is the page that comes up when you click "home" when you are on the Internet. Or you can call the ISP and ask.)

- Do you have the filtering program for your computer(s) at home? If not, talk to your parents about getting one.

Directions: Use the maze to find your way to a safe chat room. The road blocks (filters) will stop you from going the wrong way.

Take the mouse around the road blocks

KIDS' SAFE SITES

Rules for Staying Safe in Cyberspace

Directions: Fill in the blanks, then check your answers with those below. After you have checked your answers, put these rules by your computer. Keep them there to remind you how to stay safe while using the Internet.

- Never give out any _____ information on the Internet.

- Never send pictures of _____ to anyone on the Internet without your parents' permission.

- Never arrange to meet someone _____ you have met on the Internet without your parents' permission.

- Tell your parents immediately if you ever talk to someone or see something that makes you feel _____ while using the Internet.

- Do not _____ to anyone who makes you feel uncomfortable in chat rooms or emails.

- Check with your parents and discuss what you will be doing before going _____ .

Answers:
personal
yourself
face-to-face
uncomfortable
respond
online

91

Let's Show 'Em What You've Learned

Directions: Complete the word puzzle below by filling in the missing word(s) in the sentence.

Across

1. An _____ person may make you feel uncomfortable.
2. We call a danger sign a _____ _____.
3. Someone _____ at you too long is a red flag.
4. Being alone in the _____ is a red flag.
5. I will keep a distance of at least 10 _____ from strangers.
6. The _____ _____ will stay a secret between my parents and me.
7. I will not give information over the _____.
8. I could throw things in an attacker's _____.
9. If someone tries to grab me, I should _____ loudly.
10. If someone tries to grab me, I should _____ fast.
11. If someone tries to grab me, I can _____ low.
12. In an emergency, I could _____ 911.
13. I need to be able to _____ myself to get help from a stranger.
14. __nternet __ervice __rovider.
15. _____ help block unsafe websites.

(See the correct answers on page 96.)

Down

1. An unsafe person could be driving _____.
2. Being _____ in a public place is a red flag.
3. Someone making you _____ uncomfortable is a red flag.
4. An adult that doesn't _____ in your area is a red flag.
5. A stranger _____ toward you is a red flag.
6. Parking in a _____ area is a red flag.
7. I must always try to _____ a red flag.
8. If someone tries to touch me in areas that are normally covered by a bathing suit, I will say _____.
9. I will not be fooled by the familiarity _____.
10. I will keep the outside doors _____ when I am home alone.
11. If I need help, I should go to a _____ _____ adult.
12. If someone I know tries to hurt me, I will _____ a trusted adult.
13. I will use my _____ safety rules when going online.

Resources for the Family and Community

In Print

- Finkelhor, D., K. J. Mitchell, and J. Wolak. *Online Victimization: A Report on the Nation's Youth.* National Center for Missing and Exploited Children, 2000.

- The National Center for Missing and Exploited Children publishes a variety of materials that can be useful to your family and community. You may contact them at:

  National Center for Missing and Exploited Children
  Charles B. Wang International Children's Building
  699 Prince Street
  Alexandria, Virginia 22314-3175
  1-800-843-5678 (1-800-THE-LOST)

- *A Very Touching Book* by Jan Hindman is a great resource for explaining the different types of touching to children. It was published in 1985 by Alexandria Associates, P.O. Box 87, Baker City, Or 97814, 541-523-4574.

- Anna Salter, a psychologist who has been studying sex offenders for many years, wrote an enlightening—enlightening is an understatement—book titled *Predators, Pedophiles, Rapists, and Other Sex Offenders: Who They Are, How They Operate, and How We Can Protect Ourselves and Our Children*, Basic Books, 2003. If you want to learn more about sex offenders, this is the book to read.

On the Web

- www.cybertipline.com—You can report incidences that occur involving the Internet at this site.

- www.kidsafe.com—This website is full of general safety information for your family.

- www.NetSmartz.org—This website is filled with activities for your children to learn to be safe on the Internet.

- www.rainn.org—This website has information for victims of sexual assault and their families.

- www.yellodyno.com—This website offers school programs for elementary students that deal with sexual abuse and abduction.

Other Important Things

We also highly recommend you obtain a printed list of sex offenders in your area. You may be able to download this list off of the Internet under the *sex offender registry* for your state. Unfortunately, not all states post their sex offender registries on the Internet, so you may need to contact your local law enforcement agency to find out how to obtain this information for your area.

To report information regarding a missing or sexually exploited child, call your local law enforcement agency. Then call the National Center for Missing and Exploited Children's 24-hour toll-free hotline: 1-800-THE-LOST (1-800-843-5678).

(Statistical information within this book obtained from the U.S. Department of Justice, Bureau of Justice Statistics; National Center for Missing and Exploited Children publications; and the websites listed above.)

About the Authors

Master *Jerry Hyde* began his martial arts training in Salinas, California, under Staff Sergeant Marvin Heath. He trained in both the Korean martial arts of Tang Soo Do and Tae Kwon Do. Master Hyde received his 7th degree black belt in Tang Soo Do in 2000. He was also given the rank of 7th degree black belt in Kajukenbo in 2003. He has had the privilege of training with a number of Filipino martial artists over the past 20 years. Within the Filipino martial arts, he saw a unique self-defense system that men, women, and children could use effectively, regardless of age or size.

He has been teaching this system of self-defense to his students ever since. This system not only incorporates the physical elements of self-defense, but the more important aspects of awareness, avoidance, and escape. These latter characteristics are what people commonly refer to as being "street smart." Master Hyde's longtime desire was to give this knowledge to more children than he could reach within his own school. He dreamed of writing a book that could be shared with thousands of children. So he began to place his knowledge, his expertise, and his street smarts down on paper.

Terra Hulse is one of Master Hyde's black belt students and a certified self-defense instructor. Outside of working as a registered nurse in the emergency room and being a mom, she spends her time teaching women and children self-defense. Terra also recognized the vast majority of children within her classes had little knowledge of how to protect themselves from the tactics of sexual predators. Furthermore, she discovered the books available on the topic were either written for parents or as simplistic picture books for children.

Together, Master Hyde and Terra have developed this invaluable resource for children. Their goal is to give children specific, practical, and effective techniques to protect themselves from dangerous people.

Child Survival Skills Workshops

Terra Hulse and Jerry Hyde provide kids' workshops and adult group instruction based on their book, *Child Survival Skills: How to Detect and Avoid Dangerous People.* They also speak to companies, association, schools, and organizations. If you are interested in bringing their expertise to your community, please contact them at:

Bentle Books
P.O. Box 2274 • Oakhurst, CA 93644
1-800-318-5741
terra@bentlebooks.com • jerry@bentlebooks.com

Give the Gift of
Child Survival Skills
to Your Friends and Colleagues

CHECK YOUR LEADING BOOKSTORE OR ORDER HERE

❏ **YES**, I want _____ copies of *Child Survival Skills* at $14.95 each, plus $4.95 shipping per book (California residents please add $1.08 sales tax per book). Canadian orders must be accompanied by a postal money order in U.S. funds. Allow 15 days for delivery.

My check or money order for $_____ is enclosed.

Please charge my: ❏ Visa   ❏ MasterCard

Name _____

Organization _____

Address _____

City/State/Zip _____

Phone_____ E-mail _____

Card # _____

Exp. Date_____ Signature _____

Please make your check payable and return to:
Bentle Books
P.O. Box 2274 • Oakhurst, CA 93644

Call your credit card order to: 1-800-318-5741

Order online at **www.BentleBooks.com**

For bulk orders and questions email sales@BentleBooks.com

Let's Show 'Em What You've Learned

Correct answers to the crossword puzzle on page 92.

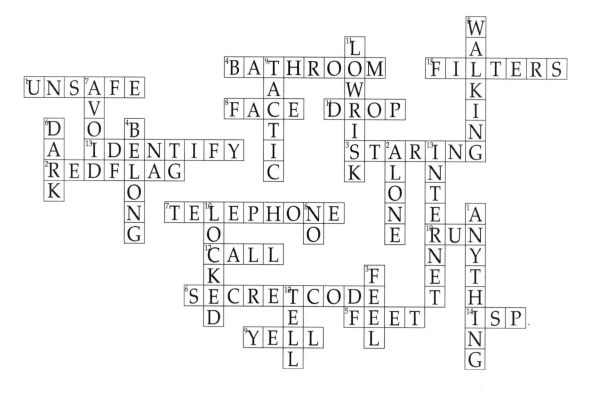